# Keeping Our Promises

## How To Be
## A Guilt-Free Mother

Stephanie Moyer Seigh

ISBN  1-4414-9240-2

EAN-13  9781441492401

This book is dedicated
with love and a humble heart
to mothers everywhere...
and to the children
whose lives they touch.

Ten percent of all profits from

Keeping Our Promises

is donated to organizations
that support the needs of
women and children.

# Contents

# Acknowledgments

Thank you to...

my parents, Donna Killian, Don Moyer, Brenda Moyer and Lee Killian. In the African tradition, when *thank you* isn't enough, they say, "I give you life." Thank you for giving me life... and now I give it back to you.

my prayer partners, Revs. Pat Bessey, Audrey Bickford, Ann Marie Acacio and Judi Venturini. Thank you for holding the high watch and knowing the truth of me, especially when I would forget.

the teachers who came when the student was ready, Nancy LeRoy and Maria Nemeth. I would not be the person I am today without you.

Unity of Lehigh Valley, for your love and support during the writing of this book, and for making me a better coach, minister, friend and mother.

Marguerite Chandler and Shirley Frederick, for their loving and thorough editing.

my coach, Carole Rehbock, and our therapists, Vickie Parker and Jane Stover, for helping me to cross the border, seeing how important this book was to me, and not letting me give up.

the teachers I have never met and whose impact on my life has been immeasurable, Marianne Williamson, Gene Roddenberry, Kahlil Gibran and George Lucas. Your wisdom has opened my eyes, my mind and my heart; your courage has inspired me.

our animals, Tasha, Lucky, Ginger, Sadie, Spike, Sophie and Max. For teaching me what unconditional love really looks like.

my children, Jon, Collin and Jackie. I love you more than life. Thank you for helping me learn the importance of keeping my promises.

and finally, to my husband, Ken. Words are inadequate to express my gratitude and love. How fortunate I am among women. Til the end of time...

# Introduction

*"Though no one can go back and make a brand new start, my friend, anyone can start from now to make a brand new end."*
*~ Carl Bard*

This book grew out of a quote I found on a calendar: *Learn from the mistakes of others. You can't live long enough to make them all on your own.* As the mother of three, I have made more than my fair share of mistakes. And as is typical of most of the mothers I know, I tend to dwell on my failures more than my successes. Since I am an optimistic person by nature, I wondered if perhaps my mistakes might be of benefit to those young women, or not so young women, just starting out on this adventure we call "motherhood."

The original title of this book was *True Confessions of a Guilt-Ridden Mother,* but two events caused me to change my mind. First, there was the high school graduation of our oldest son, Jonathan. For reasons I'll explain later, Jon lived with his father, my ex-husband, for the last three years of high school.

This was a difficult decision. And, when it came time for Jon to graduate, I grieved. This grief was unexpected and disconcerting. I had expected that this would be a joyful time, especially given Jon's difficulty with school. But instead, I spent the week preceding his graduation in a kind of mourning for what could have been, if I had only been a "better," more perfect, mother.

Flash forward three months to an episode of Oprah, with special guest, Gwyneth Paltrow. The interview took place shortly after the birth of her daughter, Apple. At one point during the show, Gwyneth turned to Oprah and asked why it was that all mothers felt guilty. She laughingly explained that no matter how much time she spent with her daughter, if she even left her for an hour for an exercise class, she felt guilty, and wondered if all mothers felt that way.

I found myself nodding an emphatic "Yes!" to her question, which led me to ask, "Why?" Why is it that even the "best" mothers, the most well-intentioned of us, feels guilty? Is it in our DNA? Could it be our sometimes ridiculous expectations of ourselves to be superwomen? Or can we blame society? I sometimes envy the women in my mother's generation, when the roles were so much clearer, albeit more restrictive. Yes, as women, we have much more freedom than our mothers and grandmothers, and as always, that freedom comes with a price. In this case, I believe the cost is frequently our peace of mind, as we question our every decision, doubting not only our competence as mothers, but as wives, daughters and even friends.

So the question became for me, in part, how can we feel "enough"? How can we support one another, through sharing our mistakes and our successes, our joys and our triumphs, into seeing that we truly are doing our best in every situation? How can we support one another into really enjoying our lives, and our relationships, with a minimum of "shoulds" and guilt?

As I explored these questions, I was reminded of the nature of promises. When we make a promise, we enter into a state of tension that is only relieved when we fulfill the promise. This is why we frequently feel joy, or at the very least relief, when we fulfill a commitment, or keep a promise - we are releasing the tension caused by entering into the agreement. David Allen reflects this phenomenon with this observation: *Much of the stress that people feel doesn't come from having too much to do. It comes from not finishing what they started.*

So, what if our "mother guilt" is based on this tension? Could it be that we believe we made certain promises upon becoming mothers that we cannot possibly fulfill, thereby keeping us in a constant state of tension?  And, would it be possible to simplify and quantify these promises, so that we can in fact attain them and feel the joy that so often accompanies a promise kept? I believe the answer to both of these questions is, "Yes."  Yes, we can learn to shift from guilt-ridden to guilt-free and ultimately, joyous, mothering.

*Keeping Our Promises* has evolved out of my own journey, my mistakes and successes, and my own growth as the mother of three amazing human beings. What started out as a predominantly academic exercise has turned into an incredibly healing exploration of the very nature of guilt itself and what it actually means to be a "mother."

The Buddha teaches, "We are what we think. All that we are arises with our thoughts. With our thoughts we make the world." I invite you to join with me as we learn to make and keep these sweet, simple promises... and make the world a more joyous place for ourselves and our families.

*Stephanie Moyer Seigh*
*February 2009*

# On Children

And a woman who held a babe against her bosom said, Speak to us of Children. And he said:

Your children are not your children.

They are the sons and daughters of Life's longing for itself.

They come through you but not from you,

And though they are with you yet they belong not to you.

You may give them your love but not your thoughts,

For they have their own thoughts.

You may house their bodies but not their souls,

For their souls dwell in the house of tomorrow, which you cannot visit, not even in your dreams.

You may strive to be like them, but seek not to make them like you.

For life goes not backward nor tarries with yesterday.

You are the bows from which your children as living arrows are sent forth.

The archer sees the mark upon the path of the infinite, and He bends you with His might that His arrows may go swift and far.

Let your bending in the archer's hand be for gladness;

For even as He loves the arrow that flies, so He loves also the bow that is stable.

*Kahlil Gibran, "The Prophet"*

# The Guilt-Ridden Mother

*"There is only one courage and that is the courage to go on dying to the past, not to collect it...*
*not to cling to it. We all cling to the past, and because we cling to the past we become unavailable to the present."*
*~ Bhagwan Shree Rajneesh*

A student went to his master and asked, "Master, what is the secret to happiness?" And the master replied, "Good judgment." Then the student asked, "Master, how does one obtain good judgment?" And the master replied, "Experience." Then the student asked, "Master, how does one get this experience?" And the master replied, "Bad judgment."

We laugh at this, almost despite ourselves, because it is true. Samuel Smiles wrote, "We learn wisdom from failure much more than from success; we often discover what will do, by finding out what will not do; and probably he who never made a mistake never made a discovery." And Eileen Caddy teaches us that, "Regrets can hold you back and can prevent the most wonderful things taking place in our lives."

We learn from our mistakes. This truth is accepted as universal. So why do we berate ourselves for making those mistakes? We lie awake at night, obsessing over what we should have done, or shouldn't have done. We cling to the past, and allow our regrets to hold us back, by becoming fearful of making more mistakes.

I am not an expert on parenting. I do not have a Ph.D. in child rearing, or anything else. I have done some things well, and some things not so well. I have been patient, and I have lost my temper. I have been wise, and I have been exceedingly foolish. I have been kind and I have been cruel. In the end, I am simply a mother who has tried to do her best and has had her share of failures.

And I have also had my share of successes. What has made the difference? What is the common denominator, the deciding factor, between the failures and the successes? I believe it is the quality of our promises, and the clarity of the expectations behind those promises. I heard once that guilt and resentment are flip sides of the same coin, and the coin is unrealized expectations. What expectations have we had of ourselves, and of our children, that contribute to our experience, perceived or real, of failure?

My friend Connie sent me an interesting excerpt from a 1950's Home Economics textbook intended for high school girls, entitled, "How to prepare for married life":

1. Have dinner ready: Plan ahead, even the night before, to have a delicious meal, on time. This is a way of letting him know that you have been thinking about him, and are concerned about his needs. Most men are hungry when they come home and the prospects of a good meal are part of the warm welcome needed.

2. Prepare yourself: Take 15 minutes to rest so you will be refreshed when he arrives. Touch up your make-up, put a ribbon in your hair and be fresh looking. He has just been with a lot of work-weary people. Be a little gay and a little more interesting. His boring day may need a lift.

3. Clear away the clutter: Make one last trip through the main part of the house just before your husband arrives, gathering up school books, toys, paper, etc. Then run a dust cloth over the tables. Your husband will feel he has reached a haven of rest and order, and it will give you a lift too.

4. Prepare the children: Take a few minutes to wash the children's hands and faces if they are small, comb their hair, and if necessary, change their clothes. They are little treasures and he would like to see them playing the part.

5. Minimize the noise: At the time of his arrival, eliminate all noise of washer, dryer, dishwasher, or vacuum. Try to encourage the children to be quiet. Be happy to see him. Greet him with a warm smile and be glad to see him.

6. Some DON'TS: Don't greet him with problems or complaints. Don't complain if he's late for dinner. Count this as minor compared with what he might have gone through that day.

7. Make him comfortable: Have him lean back in a comfortable chair or suggest he lie down in the bedroom. Have a cool or warm drink ready for him.

Arrange his pillow and offer to take off his shoes. Speak in a low, soft, soothing and pleasant voice. Allow him to relax and unwind.

8. Listen to him: You may have a dozen things to tell him, but the moment of his arrival is not the time. Let him talk first.

9. Make the evening his: Never complain if he does not take you out to dinner or to other places of entertainment; instead try to understand his world of strain and pressure and his need to be home and relax.

10. The Goal: Try to make your home a place of peace and order where your husband can relax.

I found this interesting in several ways. It helped to explain the Donna Reed/June Cleaver phenomenon of the 1950's and 60's. The perfect wife, and mother, lived for her family. Their needs were paramount, her needs secondary. And everybody played their part, even the children - *They (the children) are little treasures and he would like to see them playing the part.* Most interesting to me was that it was obviously the mother's role to make sure the children "played the part." The question to ask here is: What was their part? And is it any wonder that the 1970's brought us the sexual revolution and bra burning?

To be fair, there is a certain simplicity, and clarity, of the role definition inherent in the family structure of the era in which that textbook was published. But at what cost? How long can a system, a society, thrive and flourish when the family structure is so one-sided? If we are to believe Confucius, there cannot be harmony in the home when there is not beauty in the person, and that beauty grows from the light in our souls. Too often, the unrealistic and lopsided expectations of our society have dimmed, if not extinguished, the light in our souls. And this is particularly true of the light in the souls of our children.

I believe, in reaction to those expectations, and in our zeal to experience life outside of the home, we thought we could do it all - have a full-time career and live up to society's expectations of the perfect wife and mother - a beautifully coifed, size 8, with a spotless home, perfect children, a happy husband, and dinner on the table every night.

We were to work all day, not just at any job, but a career with meaning, and still be home in time to make dinner, help the children with their homework, do the laundry, volunteer with the PTA, bake cookies for school functions, host lavish birthday parties... and be attentive and supportive of our husbands who, after all, had the "important" jobs and needed to rest when they came home. We tried to be all things to all people at all times. And we were exhausted.

> "There is more to life than increasing its speed."
> ~ Gandhi

It took years, but eventually we began to realize that having it all was not only impossible, but undesirable. Bette Midler once remarked that she didn't want it all - there wasn't enough room! And Joan Lunden observed that the term "working mother" was an oxymoron - *every* mother is a working mother. Slowly, we began to see that "women's lib" was really "people's lib." The goal wasn't just to liberate women from unfair, unreasonable, and oppressive expectations, but to also liberate men from their own set of frequently restrictive societal obligations.

We began to see more and more men taking responsibility for household chores and child care, and spending less time at the office. We began to see a shift in priorities, from driven behavior to a more balanced perspective on life. Role definitions have started to soften and blur, away from his and her, to personality and talent-driven choices. My husband and I are a good example of this. He is the chief cook and shopper. I love yard work and paying the bills. Some of our roles are more traditional - I do the laundry, he takes care of the cars. But even here, these choices were determined by what we enjoy doing, not by society's definitions of "girl jobs" and "boy jobs."

> *"Guilt is the tension you feel to change your past, present or future for someone else's sake. It's your tension, you can let it go."*
> *~ Richard Bach*

By all appearances, we are slowly but surely gaining a more balanced perspective on our relationships, our careers and our families. So why are we still guilt-ridden mothers? Why, for all our gains in equal standing, do mothers still feel an unrelenting sense of responsibility for their children's happiness and well-being?

I adore my husband. We married when my three children were still in car seats, and he has raised them as his own. I thought for years that he didn't lie awake at night worrying because he was a stepfather. I was at my hairdresser's one day, getting my "natural" blonde touched up, and I asked Tina for her opinion on the subject. "Does Ken not obsess over his decisions because he's a stepfather or a man?" Without hesitation, she replied, "Because he's a man!" Women in adjoining chairs chimed in their agreement. The consensus was that no matter how involved a father is in raising his children - and most of the women there agreed that their husbands were very involved - they just didn't feel the guilt, the regret, the remorse, sometimes the outright shame that women feel over their "bad judgment."

It would take another book to explore why men, for the most part, don't share in the guilt that mothers experience. Maybe it's societal, maybe genetic, maybe a combination of both. I know from personal experience that my husband does not "fret" over his decisions regarding the children. It's not that he doesn't care about the children's well-being. On the contrary, he is very involved in their lives and supportive of their activities and dreams. He just doesn't appear to feel personally responsible for their happiness, or to blame himself if they're not. In short, he is not guilt-ridden.

In discussing our seemingly universal guilt with other women, I have seen varying degrees of regret, some anger and resentment, resignation, frustration and many tears. I have also seen a sincere desire to let go of the guilt, to stop clinging to the past, to our mistakes, to move on and start enjoying our families. And the question I have heard most frequently is, "How? How do we do that?"

I believe the answer lies in clarifying and simplifying what is expected of us, or, more accurately, what we expect of ourselves. Are we responsible for our children's happiness and well-being, both present and future? Or, as we read in

Gibran's masterpiece, *On Children*, are we willing to allow our children to come through us and not belong to us? Are we willing to give them our love and allow them to have their own thoughts, their own dreams and their own tomorrows?

A group of friends were sharing "mom" stories one afternoon. One mother moaned, "I wonder if I did *it* today?" Another mother asked her what "it" was. "The thing that will totally screw up my kid," she replied. I laughed ruefully when I heard this story. Many times I have agonized over a harsh word or a lost temper; over forgetting a dentist appointment or being late for a school play; over being too tired for a bedtime story or anything more than macaroni and cheese out of the box for dinner. Any one of these incidents could have been "it" - any one of these incidents could have permanently "screwed up my kids" and placed me on the Bad Mother List forever.

Or could they? As I contemplated our ability to influence our children, I became aware of a thin layer of arrogance underneath this belief. There have been many debates over nature vs. nurture, over our biological tendencies vs. our upbringing. Proponents

12

of both sides claim precedence, that our genes dictate our behavior and our upbringing has very little to do with it. Or the opposite, that how we are raised can override any genetic disposition.

I find myself in the middle of this debate. I have three children, born very closely together, raised by the same three parents, and all very different. Do I see myself in them? Yes, both in the color of their eyes and

> "Your children are not your children. They are the sons and daughters of Life's longing for itself. They come through you but not from you, and though they are with you yet they belong not to you."
> ~ Kahlil Gibran

to some extent in how they view the world. But they are unique individuals, in many ways very different from their parents and their grandparents. Is it arrogant to presume that as their mother I can "mold" them to such an extent that they could deny their reason for being, their soul's desire?

Are we willing to recognize that our children are not us? That they are not our second chance at life, or our opportunity to do it "right," whatever "right" means? How different would our lives be, our families be, if we operated under the assumption that our children have a reason for being that is distinctly their own, and that our job, our responsibility, is not to mold them to *our* expectations, or society's expectations, but simply to care for them so they are able to fulfill *their* promise.

If this is true, if our children do not belong to us, then what is our responsibility to them? How do we define our role as "parent" and more specifically, "mother"?

The dictionary defines the word *mother* as a woman who has given birth or a female parent; the cause or source of anything; a woman in authority. As a verb, *to mother* means to adopt or care for. So a mother is a female parent who cares for her children. It's that simple... and yet we make it so hard. We buy into the "shoulds" that are passed from one mother to another; to the black-and-white perfect television mothers of the 50's and 60's; and to society's expectations that unless our children are reading by age 4 and soccer pros by age 7, we must be doing something wrong.

I remember one morning many years ago being on the phone with my mother. I was recently separated with three very young children and holding down three part time jobs (more about this later). I was exhausted, both from the physical exertion of the schedule I was keeping and the guilt I was heaping upon myself for the divorce and subsequent disruption to my children's lives. My mother remarked that my grandmother used to stay up until 2:00 in the morning starching her curtains, and never complained about being tired.

At the time, I remember being too exhausted to even respond, but later became angry at the comparison. Here I was trying to keep a roof over my children's heads and put food on their table, and I was being criticized for not having starched curtains! I realize now that my anger was a result of my guilt, my feeling "wrong," and my perception that the other women in my family always had their act together, as if there is such a thing.

Today, I see my mother's comment as a reflection of her discomfort. My mother is one of the most loving and compassionate women I know. It must have been hard for her to see her daughter, and grandchildren, suffering. She simply didn't know how to help me or to deal with her own feelings of frustration regarding my situation.

Thinking back to this interaction, which obviously made an impression even through my sleep deprivation and lack of focus at the time, I could see the countless times where my interactions with my own children have gone badly, not because of their behavior, but out of *my* discomfort, *my* guilt. Because the truth is, guilt is all about *us*. Guilt's focus is not on how we can best serve those that we love, but on how miserable we are capable of becoming. Guilt keeps us firmly rooted in the past, and firmly focused on ourselves. When we are willing to let it go, to learn our lessons with grace, to do our best and then move on, only then are we able to truly care for our children. Only when we have the courage to die to our past can we become available to our children in the present.

*"The parents have eaten sour grapes
and the children's teeth are set on edge."*
*~ Proverbs*

In my travels, both geographic and of a more spiritual nature, I have been exposed to many cultures and belief systems. Throughout these pages, I will share wisdom that has helped me, both personally and professionally, from many faith traditions. Coming from a Judeo-Christian background, I am most familiar with Biblical references, but have also been drawn to and fed by many Eastern paths, including the teachings of Buddha, Lao-Tzu and more contemporary teachers. Many of these paths have visited the concept of familial guilt, as illustrated by the above teaching from Proverbs.

For centuries, the belief that the sins of parents were visited upon their children perpetuated the concept of "inherited guilt." Another example of this teaching can be found in Deuteronomy 23:2: "Those born of an illicit union shall not be admitted to the assembly of the Lord. Even to the tenth generation, none of their descendants shall be admitted..."

Interestingly, this directive intended to indict children for the crimes of their parents was softened in the next chapter. Deuteronomy 24:16 reads,

"Parents shall not be put to death for their children, nor shall children be put to death for their parents; only for their own crimes may persons be put to death." An extreme example, granted, but an example nevertheless that we are only responsible for our own actions, and not those of the generations that precede us.

In Ezekiel 18, the prophet shares this revelation: "The word of the Lord came to me: What do you mean by repeating this proverb concerning the land of Israel, 'The parents have eaten sour grapes, and the children's teeth are set on edge'? As I live, says the Lord GOD, this proverb shall no more be used by you in Israel. Know that all lives are mine; the life of the parent as well as the life of the child is mine: it is only the person who sins that shall die."

What a gift! In this one short passage, we are absolved of the "sins" of the generations that came before us and begin to see a shift in the root and causes of guilt. Here, we are absolved of the guilt that is so frequently passed from one generation to another. And yet, how often we choose to hold on to that guilt, and, in fact, to perpetuate it unto the next

18

generation. We do it very subtly. We no longer literally put our children to death for the sins of their parents, but we are very capable of killing their spirits by imposing upon them the dysfunction of generations of blame, shame and judgment that poison our families.

This is rarely conscious. We don't wake up in the morning and declare, "Today I'm going to make the same mistakes my parents did. Today I'm going to perpetuate the dysfunction of the generations that preceded me." We react out of our conditioning, out of the way "things have always been done." And that's the problem. It's time for us to wake up, to stop creating out of our guilt, out of our "shoulds," and start creating out of the Truth of who we are – the strong, loving, wise, intuitive, caring mothers that we are all capable of being. The mothers we were born to be.

Keeping these seven promises can help us to do just that. From the first – *We Promise to be Present* – to the last – *We Promise to Forgive* – these promises take us on a journey of releasing our guilt and focusing our attention on how we can truly, deeply serve our children and our families, while loving and caring for ourselves. For the two must go together. When we ignore the yearnings of our own soul's desire, our need to heal and forgive, to express the Truth of who we are, we are incapable of caring for anyone else. Keeping these seven promises takes us from confused to clear, from self-centered to selfless, and ultimately from guilt-ridden to joyous. There is no greater gift we can give to our children.

# The First Promise:

## We promise to be present.

*"A hundred years from now... it will not matter what my bank account was, the sort of house I lived in, or the kind of car I drove. But the world may be different because I was important in the life of a child."*
*~ Author Unknown*

When I left my first husband (I always hesitate to say "first," as that implies there is, or will be, a series of husbands, which is not true and, God willing, won't be true), I had three children under four years old, and was still nursing my 5-month-old daughter. As I received little  child support for the first couple of years after my divorce, I had a choice to make.  I could either work 2-3 part time jobs, as daycare was not in the budget, relying on family, friends and babysitters to help me care for the children.  Or I could apply for public assistance.  I chose the former. If I had to do it again, I would choose the latter.

What does it mean to promise to be present? Simply put, when we are being present, we are in the moment. We're not obsessing about the past or worrying about the future, or mentally going over our to-do list. We are right here, in the moment, right now.

My children have become acutely aware of when I am not present. Several years ago, when my son Collin was in elementary school, we were having a conversation in the car on the way home from soccer practice. At one point, he turned to me and said, "Mom, you're not listening. You've just said, 'Great, Collin' three times in a row and I don't think you've actually heard what I said." Ouch. At first I protested, and smugly repeated back to him what he had been relating. But later, I realized that what he had observed was true - I was hearing him, but I wasn't listening. I wasn't present to his need to be truly, deeply heard, not with my ears, but with my heart. What he was really saying to me was, "Mom, I need to be your priority in this moment. Pay attention to me."

Buddhists refer to this presence as mindfulness. Jon Kabat Zinn defines mindfulness as moment-to-moment awareness. "It is cultivated by refining our capacity to pay attention, intentionally, in the present moment, and then sustaining that attention over time as best we can. In the process, we become more in touch with our life as it is unfolding." What I find interesting, and immensely helpful, about mindfulness is that it keeps us out of guilt. Think about it - guilt is always about the past. Being mindful keeps us centered in the present, in what is happening right now. We don't deny our mistakes, but are willing to learn from them and move on. I saw a church marquee once that said, "The present contains many gifts - be willing to untie the box."

Inherent in this promise is the need to prioritize. When we make something a priority, we say that, in that moment, there is nothing more important. We will not be distracted from our task, our goal. We might say that we are single-minded in our focus. When we make our family a priority, in the moment we make that decision, nothing is more important.

This does not mean that our families will *always* be our priority. This is perhaps the most guilt-inducing belief held by mothers everywhere: That our family must *always* be our priority. More doubt, more regret, and more anguish have been wrought by the misguided belief that our families must always be the focus of our attention, even to the exclusion of our personal needs being met. However, when we do choose to make our family a priority, then we must do just that: Make them *the* priority.

In establishing that in this moment nothing is more important, we are giving them the gift of our attention. We could say that when we make our families our priority, we have no other idols before us. Many books have been written about the concept of idols in our modern society. An idol can be anything that distracts us from our purpose or causes us to lose sight of the truth of who we are, anything we worship that does not support full authenticity.

> *"You shall not make for yourself an idol, whether in the form of anything that is in heaven above, or that is on the earth beneath, or that is in the water under the earth. You shall not bow down to them or worship them."*
> ~ Exodus

Common examples of idols are money, power, sex and fame. The more mundane variety of idols include television, video games, substance abuse, and any activity taken to excess.

For our purposes, we will define an "idol" as anything that prevents us from giving our full attention to our current priority. To that end, I will confess that I am affectionately known in our home as the resident "vidiot." When the television is on, I'm gone. My husband has observed that I take on a kind of glazed look when engrossed in a television program. I can also get so lost in a good book that I am literally deaf to conversation around me, even conversation directed towards me! In moderation, neither of these is necessarily a "bad" thing. One might even say they show a propensity for sustained concentration. And if the priority for the evening is to watch a movie or favorite program, they are even appropriate.

Where I get into trouble is when they're not the priority, but are in fact distracting me from what's most important. To return to our definition, they are preventing me from giving my full attention to my current priority. So, when I am writing, the television is turned off. I don't start reading a book unless I know I will have time to finish it without interfering with a previous commitment. And when my family is my priority, they get my full attention.

*"Hindsight is 20/20."*

So why, in retrospect, would I have gone on public assistance after leaving my first marriage? Because my children were my priority and I got distracted by an idol. The idol wasn't work, or putting a roof over their heads, or even protecting them from an angry (at the time) ex-husband. The idol that prevented me from giving my children the full attention they needed at that time was *my pride.*

I was the product of a solidly middle-class family, had a college degree, kept my children clean, clothed and fed, and had created a beautiful home. I was not the "type" of woman to go on public assistance. Furthermore, no one in my family had ever needed that type of help. We were proud of our self-reliance and ability to pull ourselves up by our bootstraps, no matter how desperate the circumstances. So I chose to allow my children to be juggled between caregivers while I exhausted myself by running between jobs. This was not good for my children and it was not good for me. It was a mistake.

I have since learned that public assistance is precisely for people "like me." It was originally designed to help people who were temporarily in need, as a means of helping them get back on their feet, metaphorically speaking, until they could once again reach independence.

I did make a good decision at that time which required only a minimum of pride-swallowing. I applied for and received WIC (Women, Infants and Children). This is a wonderful program that gives food coupons to mothers of young children, and even more to nursing mothers of young children, which I was at the time. The coupons are good for specific foods, of the healthy, low-sugar, variety. I would leave the grocery store with several full bags of groceries for a very small amount of money. It literally saved my life during that first year of single motherhood.

*"Why is a working plumber someone who works
as a plumber, a working doctor someone who works
as a doctor, but a working mother only someone
who works at something else?"*
~ *Naomi Barko*

Another idol that can distract us from our priorities is the "What will people think?" idol, or the idol of public opinion. The specter of being a neglectful mother looms large in our society, more or less so depending on how you define "neglectful."

The dictionary defines *neglect* as to give too little care or attention to; to leave undone or not attend to; to omit or fail. To be *neglectful* is to be careless; negligent; heedless. Notice the wording in the first definition: to give *too little* care or attention to. As guilt-ridden mothers, we can frequently feel neglectful if we don't give ALL our care or attention to our children, ALL the time.

It's time that we adjusted that expectation. It's not only OK, but healthy to have other priorities occasionally. We need to stop judging ourselves as neglectful when we indulge in a bubble bath with the bathroom door *locked*. Or give the children TV dinners while we go out to dinner with girlfriends. Or even to miss the occasional school event because we have an opportunity for career advancement in another state.

Let's be clear. This promise is not meant to rationalize real neglect or abuse. None of the promises are intended to help us justify truly poor behavior. As parents, it is our responsibility to see to the physical and emotional needs of our children. The intention of this promise is to help us keep our priorities in order, without guilt or judgment, and to keep our focus on what's most important *in this moment...*to be present to the real needs of our children.

Like many women of my generation, I believe that natural consequences are better teachers than punishment. Allowing our children to experience the natural consequences of their actions, rather than punishing them for misbehaving, can sometimes look neglectful from the outside. My friend Donna related this classic story from when her very active son was young:

"I remember one day I had to go grocery shopping for four essential items: eggs, milk, bread and American cheese. I was pretty wiped that day and warned my son that if he ran off, as he was likely to do, no matter where we were and what was left to do, I would leave it all and we would go home without any eggs, milk, bread or cheese. We no sooner got into the store when he bolted. I got him by the hand and he looked up and said, 'I blew it didn't I?'

We left, and when he got home and asked for milk, there was none and when he wanted a grilled cheese sandwich, I told tell him we didn't have the bread or the cheese. As young as he was, he got the message. Grocery shopping was a little easier after that."

From the outside, this could look like a mother neglecting her child's nutritional needs, but Donna saw a teaching opportunity and took it, regardless of how it might have made her look. In that moment, the needs of her child took precedence over how good or bad a mother she was appearing to be. She was more interested in doing the right thing than in looking "right."

> *"Active laziness...consists of cramming our lives with compulsive activity, so that there is no time at all to confront the real issues...Our lives seem to live us, possess their own bizarre momentum to carry us away. In the end we feel we have no control or choice over them."*
> ~ The Tibetan Book of Living and Dying

I love lists. I make one almost every night before I go to bed and look at it over my morning coffee. Checking off the items on my list gives me a sense of tremendous accomplishment, no matter how small the task. I think lists are a good thing. I love having a list.... and I have recognized that sometimes my lists have *me*. I can become compulsive about getting something done *because it's on the list* instead of because it needs to be done. This is when prioritizing becomes a priority, because busyness can become a panacea. We can become so enamored of our list that we fail to recognize what's truly important in the moment. We fail to be mindful or to take time to "confront the real issues."

This means we need to be willing to forget

about our list if our teenage daughter comes home from school in tears. Or if our best friend calls in a panic because her teenage daughter didn't come home at all. We need to be willing to forget about our list if completing the task at hand becomes more important than the people at hand. As has been related by those nearing the end of their lives, they have rarely regretted spending less time at work, but frequently regret spending less time with their loved ones. The list can wait. Our relationships can't.

# The Second Promise:

## We promise to lighten up.

*"The words differ from one tradition to another, but their central message is the same: You are more than you think! The great religions all exist to help us discover our true Self and our true relationship to the sacred. This discovery... is the supreme joy and greatest goal of human life."* ~ *Roger Walsh*

A student once asked me to define enlightenment. I replied that I believed to become enlightened is to "lighten up," to be willing to take ourselves a little less seriously, to bring more joy and less angst to what we do and how we relate to others. In order to do this, I believe we need to recognize that our life here is a journey, a series of lessons and experiences that eventually lead to mastery - not of a specific path, but of ourselves. I believe to be fully enlightened to is to be fully authentic, fully self-aware and fully aligned with our place in the Universe.

> "Joy is the unmistakable evidence of the presence of God."
> ~ Teilhard de Chardin

From this perspective, our mistakes become opportunities for growth, for personal inquiry, not one more means by which we beat ourselves up. When we are willing to lighten up on ourselves, we naturally lighten up on others, including our children. Keeping this promise lays the foundation for a more joyful, en-lightened life.

It has been said that we are spiritual beings having a human experience. But what does this mean? In recognizing our innate spirituality, do we deny our humanity, or is the goal to fully integrate our spiritual nature and our human experience? To explore these questions, it would be helpful to explore the Perennial Philosophy. This phrase, first coined by Leibniz, a 17th century mathematician, diplomat and philosopher, was the subject of Aldous Huxley's classic *The Perennial Philosophy*. Roger Walsh, in his wonderful book *Essential Spirituality*, does a good job of describing the four assertions that are at the core of this Philosophy:

First, that underlying the physical reality in which we live and breathe and have our being is a Divine foundation, without which physical reality cannot exist. In essence, there are two realities - physical reality and spiritual reality. This spiritual reality is recognized by many names - Divine Mind, the Tao, Brahman, God, Spirit - and exists outside of time and space.

Second, we live in both realities. Inside each one of us is a Divine spark, a transcendent center, providing a connecting link between the two realities.

Third, we are capable of accessing the spirit realm, and the wisdom contained therein, by looking within ourselves. Through spiritual practices such as prayer, meditation, contemplation, yoga and journaling, to name only a few, we are able to realize our spiritual nature, which is...

Fourth, our very reason for being. Call it salvation, sartori, enlightenment, the great faith traditions agree that discovering "our true relationship to the sacred" is why we are here and in fact is the "supreme joy and greatest goal of human life."

This promise continues the process of getting

our priorities in order - and that means realizing our spiritual nature becomes more than a philosophy or an academic exercise - it becomes our top priority, our "greatest goal." It is the first step to lightening up.

*"Come apart for awhile."*
*~ Jesus*

Jesus taught us to seek first the Kingdom of Heaven, and went on to explain that the Kingdom of Heaven is within each one of us. When we access this Heaven, when we spend time with Spirit, with the Truth of who we are, we are calmer, more considerate, more joyous human beings. Science bears this out. When we meditate on a regular basis, our blood pressure goes down, our pulse slows and our minds are sharper. Taking quiet time for yourself every day is not a luxury, it is a necessity. Jesus taught us to love our neighbors *as ourselves*. Take time every day to love yourself by connecting with the Divine spark that is your essence.

When our children were very young, I consistently put my own needs at the bottom of our to-do list. I worked from home so I could be with the children, which was a wonderful idea... in theory. What we didn't take into account was that between my business, volunteering, and taking care of three young children, I was never <u>not</u> working. After repeated  encouragement from my husband to take time for myself, he reminded me of one of the cardinal rules of air travel:  *put the oxygen mask on yourself first*. (More on this later.) We don't serve our families, friends or communities by burning out, or "pulling a martyr," as my teenagers called it.

This doesn't have to be complicated or hard.  It can be as simple as spending ten minutes once or twice a day behind a closed door with your eyes closed, breathing slowly and deliberately, luxuriating in the space between breaths.  It can take the form of a walking meditation first thing in the morning or after dinner, taking in the song of the birds or a fresh snow fall... or getting wet from a warm spring rain.

Put on a favorite CD, light a candle, read from a favorite holy text, pray before an altar or sit in your garden. I once read that Goldie Hawn, when her children were young, would lock herself in the bathroom for ten minutes of quiet.  Whatever form your "quiet time" takes, just do it.

When we take time to connect with the light in our souls, we are more beautiful, inside and out. We quite literally "lighten" up.

> "When there is light in the soul, there will be beauty in the person."
> ~ Confucius

Jesus taught, "You are the light of the world... No one after lighting a lamp puts it under the bushel basket, but on the lampstand, and *it gives light to all in the house.*" In her now famous quote from *A Return to Love*, Marianne Williamson encourages us to be freed from our fears, so our presence will automatically free others from theirs. In the same way, when we are willing to shine our Light, to fully demonstrate the Truth of our being, we automatically free others to shine theirs.

Nowhere is this principle more important than in our own homes. We set no better example for our children than to be willing to share our gifts and talents with them, and the world. In a recent children's sermon, I explained that when we don't do what we're good at, it's like refusing a gift. And that's not polite.  God has given each of us gifts to share, a light to shine, and it is our privilege and our joy to do just that.

Margi, one of my teachers and a gifted coach, encourages her students and clients to just "start!" She teaches that you don't have to be good to start, but you have to start to be good. So many times our fear of doing something wrong, or of a steep learning curve, stops us from even starting. The longest journey begins with one step.  Be willing to start.

> "I have spent my days stringing and unstringing my instrument while the song I came to sing remains unsung."
> ~ Ragindranath Tagore

Children learn by watching what we do much more than by hearing what we say. Shine your light, sing the song you came here to sing... and give your child permission to do the same.  Encourage them to explore what interests them, what's fun and challenging, what keeps their attention.  These are also clues to our own gifts, areas where we can shine. Release your fear of failure, or success, and embrace your talent.

Encourage your children to embrace the Divine spark within them by accepting and nurturing their gifts, and shining their light, remembering that their light is not simply a reflection of your own. Returning to the first promise, helping our children to shine their light requires us to be present to them, to pay attention to what lights them up. This can be challenging, because what calls to them may be really foreign to us! Or conversely, their dreams can be so close to our own that we might confuse them. The gift we give to them is to be clear where their path diverges from ours, to support them with all our hearts into living their dreams - without us living through them.

Just as importantly, we need to recognize that as different as our children are from ourselves, they are also different from one another. My three children were born very close together - it was a very busy four years! And they have chosen very different paths. While Jon's passion revolves around gaming and philosophy, Collin is studying astrophysics and Jackie is pursuing a theater degree on the road to becoming a stage manager. While we can identify with bits and pieces of each of their pursuits (sci fi and theater being passions of our own!), they are clearly following their own gifts separate from, yet supported by, us.

*"To everything that has been, I say thank you.*
*To everything that will be, I say yes."*
*~ Dag Hammersjold*

As a young mother, I often struggled on the one hand with my natural tendency to be relaxed with the kids, and on the other hand with my need to provide structure and safety. An older and wiser mother shared this advice: Unless they are in danger of hurting themselves or someone else, say "yes." Save your "no's" for the big stuff. Let them explore and let them fail. Let them experience success and learn how to deal with frustration.

This sounds so easy, and yet it has been the most difficult lesson for me to learn as a mother. I so wanted to protect my children from disappointment and pain that I frequently jumped in to "save" them from their own decisions. What I finally saw was that the only thing I was saving them from was learning the lessons so critical for their growth and development. Of course, we need to be discerning here. Do we allow a toddler to run into the street? Obviously not. Do we allow a college sophomore who parked one too many times in a restricted lot to struggle with paying the towing fees? We sure do! This isn't saying "no" to helping... it's saying a big "yes" to allowing them to grow in maturity and wisdom.

This brings us full circle to our recognition that life is a journey. Much of my personal work has revolved around this recognition. So often we become obsessed with doing everything "right" - work, homemaking, parenting, marriage - as though there is a "right" way to do these things. I spent years preaching unconditional love and compassion, and yet had none for myself. While I said "yes" to my children whenever I could, my usual reply to myself was "no." What finally helped me to shift to a gentler frame of mind was recognizing that my constant self-condemnation was hurtful to my children.

This came home in a big way when my daughter was a junior in high school. We had a rule in our family that in order to participate in extra-curricular activities, grades needed to be maintained at a reasonable level. When Jackie came home with two low grades on her report card, she knew before we even spoke that she would not be allowed to stage manage the winter concert. This didn't bring either one of us any pleasure, but we both recognized the importance of keeping this agreement. At the close of our discussion, I "jokingly" placed my head in my hands, and lamented that I must be a bad mother because she had not worked up to her potential.

Later that evening, my very courageous daughter came to me in tears. She told me how painful it was to hear me speak of myself in such a negative way. She had seen through my "joking" tone to the real belief I held that I was not a good mother, that something I had done must have caused her to do poorly on her report card. She let me know in no uncertain terms that her grades had nothing to do with me, and that I was a very good mother in her eyes. And to say otherwise negated her experience with me, and her feelings.

What a powerful lesson for us both! I saw

clearly, and really for the first time, how heavily I had taken on the responsibility of mothering, and how very much I needed to lighten up. While I truly believed that this life is a wonderful adventure, my actions were not consistent with that belief. My daughter, in her wisdom, helped me to see how important it is to bring our promises into our behavior, to allow our beliefs to shape our actions, so that our thoughts, words and deeds are aligned.

I also saw how very self-focused my comment to her had been. By taking her grades as a reflection of my parenting, not only was I discounting her free will, her autonomy, I was putting the focus of the conversation on me and my parenting, instead of supporting her in looking at how she could do better in school. By moving into victim mode, I had stopped serving my daughter. It had become all about me.

And therein lies the paradox of lightening up. When we are willing to embrace the journey and acknowledge that we are simply "the bows from which our children as living arrows are sent forth," when we can learn to recognize how much of us we project onto our children, and practice being present to this moment, we become much better parents.

These are how the promises work together, not as more rules to follow, but as a process that builds upon itself. Becoming present serves as the foundation to lightening up. Once we have lightened up, discerned our true nature and learned to say yes, both to our children and ourselves, we are ready to focus on the next promise.

# The Third Promise:

## We promise to be kind.

*"Generosity lies less in giving much than in giving at the right moment."*
~ *Jean de la Bruyere*

Before we explore this promise, let's first define "kind." To be kind is to do good, be friendly; to be gentle and humane; having or showing a generous, sympathetic, considerate attitude towards others.

What a wonderful definition! Let's look more closely at generous. To be kind frequently means that we are focused on the needs and concerns of the other, that we are generous with our time and attention. It means that we withhold our judgments until all the facts are in... and then see that our judgments don't apply. Kindness says, "How can I help?" even in the face of anger or frustration, and particularly when presented with sadness or despair.

Kindness doesn't take our children's behavior personally.

Interestingly, being kind is different from being "nice," although we frequently confuse the two. Niceness is frequently an attempt on our part to be treated in a certain way, or as a means to an end. If I'm nice to you, you'll be nice to me. If I'm nice to you, you'll give me what I want, or tell me what I want to hear. Kindness, especially when seen as generosity, is not concerned with what it receives in return. In fact, real kindness sometimes is not what we would normally define as "nice." When we are truly kind, we care enough tell the truth. It may not feel nice to tell someone they have broccoli in their teeth, but it's certainly considerate and generous.

*"Sticks and stones may break my bones,*
*but words will never harm me."*

If only this were true. The truth is that words can do great harm, or great good. As parents, we have a responsibility to choose our words carefully and to never underestimate the effect a carelessly chosen word can have on our children. The Sufis recommend that we speak only after asking ourselves three questions: Is what we are about to say true? Is it necessary? Is it kind?

Sai Baba adds a fourth criteria: Does what we are about to say improve upon the silence? When we speak to our children, are we doing so out of a desire to support their education and growth, or out of a need to impress upon them the result of ours? The word education comes from the Latin *educare*, meaning to draw forth. So to educate isn't to pour information into our children as though they were an empty bucket made for us to fill, but rather it is the process of drawing forth the wisdom and innate abilities that are already found within us, within them.

> "Have reverence for all life; this manifests as unconditional love and respect for oneself and all other beings."
> ~ Taoist wisdom

We could say that when we choose our words carefully we are being respectful of the thoughts and feelings of others. When we are thoughtful in our speech, it is an indication of the esteem in which we hold ourselves and those we are in relationship with. Think about how you feel when spoken to harshly, especially by an authority figure, or someone you love or hold in high regard. The effect can be devastating. So often, we see ourselves through the eyes and actions of others, and this is particularly true of our children.

While as adults we learn to differentiate between who we are and how others see us, children do not. If children are told they are "bad," they believe they are bad, regardless of any internal evidence to the contrary. Sadly, they will continue to feel "bad" until told otherwise, and sometimes even after. Studies have shown that we tend to remember negative responses in an indirect proportion to positive ones. In other words, we need many positive "strokes" to balance even one negative comment.

*"That which you see and hear, you cannot help; but that which you say depends on you alone."*
~ Zohar

The conventional wisdom when my children were growing up was to criticize the behavior, not the child.  This was, and continues to be, good counsel. However, we still need to be cautious.  Even well-meaning criticism can have the effect of wounding our spirits.  It is important to be clear here: Are we trying to correct truly inappropriate or dangerous behavior, or are we trying to create our children in "our own image," correcting behavior that we may find offensive, but may simply be their current form of expression?  Are we being respectful in our attempts to teach our children to show respect? We've heard it before, but the wisdom bears repeating: Children learn much more from what we do than from what we say.  Actions speak louder than words.

The concept of teaching respect by showing respect reminds me of part of our earlier definition of kindness: to be considerate.  It's so easy to be terse or irritable with our kids.  I have found myself responding to my children with an impatience that I would never show to a co-worker or friend.  I think we tend to take for granted that our children will love us no matter

> "Once you label me, you negate me".
> ~Soren Kierkegaard

what, and this may very well be true. However, this assumption should never be the grounds for inconsiderate or thoughtless behavior. If we want our children to become kind, considerate and thoughtful adults, we need to treat them in the same manner.

Words, or phrases, so quickly become labels. We casually describe our children as "the slow one" or "the smart one" or "the creative one" or "the one who will never amount to anything." And just as quickly, these labels become self-fulfilling.

My father once related a story about his father that I have never forgotten. When my grandfather and his older brother were young, he overheard his parents speaking in another room. They were commenting on how Emerett, the older brother, was the smart one, and that Stanley, my grandfather, would make a good farmer. (As a side note, I also found it interesting that being a farmer, a profession that takes skill, experience, knowledge and tenacity, was somehow seen as "less than.") Emerett did in fact go on to higher education and become an Episcopal minister. My grandfather became a farmer, and eventually a factory worker for many years.

What I found amazing about this story when I heard it was that my grandfather was a very bright man. He was a bonafide Bible scholar, having educated himself through reading hundreds of books on Christianity, the Holy Land, and scriptural theses. He was also an accomplished musician, playing both the piano and the organ, and had a beautiful baritone singing voice. I remember spending countless hours in his woodworking shop, watching him create beautiful desks, cabinets, and gifts for his family. His work was exquisite. Yet in his mind, he was the "slow" one, who was supposed to stay on the farm, and would never amount to much. Despite our praise and encouragement he saw himself through his parents' eyes until his death.

Not surprisingly, this incomplete self-image had a definite effect on his own parenting. Because he could not move beyond his parents' label, despite an abundance of evidence to the contrary, he could not see the many gifts my father was born with, and frequently discouraged him from pursuing his dreams and developing his many talents. This discouragement was not malicious in nature; my

52

grandfather loved his children. He simply could not move beyond the labels that had been imposed on him. He could never acknowledge his own gifts, his own innate intelligence, and therefore was blind to those of his son, my father.

While it is clear that negative labels are counter-productive, you might ask, "What's wrong with a positive label?" Labels of any kind are destructive because eventually we stop seeing the person behind the label and only relate to the label itself. Toinette Lippe describes it this way, "We put labels on objects and people and then see them only as labels. We never actually see who or what is in front of us. Labels are a form of limitation." Labels, whether positive or negative, are limiting by their very nature, because once we've labeled someone, we tend to relate to only that aspect of who they are, rather than seeing them as a whole, multi-faceted and complex person.

Do you remember the story of the four blind men and the elephant? Four blind men were traveling in the jungle and came upon a large animal. The first man felt his trunk and said, "Surely this animal is shaped like a hose." The second man felt his leg, and said, "No, you are wrong. This animal is like a tree trunk." The third blind man felt his tail, and chided them both. "You are both wrong. This beast is shaped like a whip." And the fourth man felt his ear and laughed at the foolishness of the other three. "It is obvious that the animal is shaped like a a fan, smooth and broad."

This is what happens when we label. We become "blind" to anything other than our judgment of the other person. This can be particularly true of our children. We label a child as a "problem," and from that point on, no matter what the child does, their behavior is seen as negative, their actions suspect. Everything becomes seen, and interpreted, through the label "problem." Dr. Maria Nemeth defines this phenomenon as *characterization* and makes an interesting observation on the effect of characterization on our relationships. She says, "We don't want to be around people we've characterized because we cannot tolerate being present with our own negative thoughts and feelings. It is too uncomfortable... It's not that we don't like who *they* are; we don't like who *we* are in the presence of that person. Our negativity becomes our burden."

Interestingly, the same blindness applies to positive labels. We may avoid dealing with inappropriate behavior in our "perfect" children, because after all, *they* couldn't possibly be "bad." Perhaps a better, healthier and more truthful approach would be to simply stick to the facts when praising our children or giving them constructive feedback. As parents, we need to provide our children with both forms of feedback, without coloring that feedback with our own judgments and projections.

Obviously, this is easier said than done. This is where the two previous promises form a foundation for the third. When we are present to this moment, and not lost in our own past or our own regrets, we are able to focus our attention on the behavior occurring *in this moment.* We are able to see the behavior as part of our children's learning and growth, as part of their journey, not as a reflection of our own. We are also able to see our response as an opportunity for our own learning and growth, as an opportunity to learn from our mistakes, and the mistakes of generations before us, and parent our children in a new way... with kindness, clarity and respect.

# The Fourth Promise:

## We promise to tell the truth.

*"And the truth will set you free."*
~ *Jesus*

We promise to tell the truth. This sounds so simple. Don't we always? Well, no, not really. We tell what we *think* is the truth, what we *believe* to be the truth. But really, what we're sharing, with all good intentions, is our *opinion* about the truth. Because the truth doesn't change. Remember what we learned in Chapter Two about living in two realities? The truth is what has actually happened or not happened in physical reality, and that doesn't change according to our opinion about what has happened. We frequently confuse the two, and it is within that confusion that our suffering lies.

Let me give you an example. I struggled with writing this book for over three years. I had many reasons why it was hard. I am a very busy minister, coach, organizational consultant, wife, mother, daughter and friend. At the time of this writing, I had a long commute to church. I am on the boards of two non-profit organizations that I care deeply about. I travel extensively to other states to support churches in conflict or transition. All of this is work that I love. At home, I work closely with my husband and spend as much time with my young adult children as our schedules allow. We have multiple dogs and cats and all the love and care that goes with maintaining such a menagerie. I am very busy. That is true.

It is also true that I promised several years ago to write this book. It is a passion of mine to share the joys of parenting and to support mothers, and fathers, in releasing the guilt and societal "shoulds" that frequently impact that joy. It is my joy to share my own struggles and lessons, having been in the parenting trenches for many years, in the hope that others will learn from my mistakes, and occasional triumphs. And yet years passed and I still had not kept my promise.

Why? Because it was my *opinion* that my busy life was preventing me from writing. Every minute of busy-ness became an excuse for not writing. I was very convincing. And then I was gently supported, by my coach, husband and friends, to tell the truth. I wasn't writing my book because I wasn't writing. No drum roll. No lightening bolt of awareness. Just the simple truth. In order to write a book, you need to sit down at the computer... and write.

And so it is with the truth. Once we get to it, the way becomes clear. I needed to write. Knowing that, and being willing to be supported in doing it, took a lot less energy than coming up with one more excuse for why my busy life was keeping me from writing my book!

The same applies to how we parent our children. When we are able to move out of our opinions and projections about their actions, and simply tell the truth, the way becomes clear. Remember the old series *Dragnet*? "Just the facts, ma'am... just the facts."

on

59

To paraphrase Epictetus, it's not the experience of parenting that affects us, it's how we experience the experience. Do we see our children as extensions of

> "It's not what happens to you, but how you react to it that matters. Men are disturbed not by things, but by the view which they take of them." ~Epictetus

ourselves? Or, as we read in Gibran's piece, do we see ourselves simply as the bow from which our children fly? When our children misbehave (whatever misbehaving looks like in your house), do we immediately see it as a reflection of our parenting, or do we see it as an opportunity to educate, to draw forth from our children what is theirs to learn and to do?

The truth is, our children are not us. They are unique individuals, here to create their own lives, to contribute as only they can. Yes, they are going to make mistakes. Didn't we? The biggest gift we can give our children is *to not take their mistakes personally*. The second biggest gift is to help them learn to tell the truth too. Here the old axiom -

"children learn much more from what we do than from what we say" - becomes particularly relevant. We need to model truth-telling before we teach it.

This can take many forms. Every time we "embellish" a story to make it more interesting or exciting, we're not telling the truth. Every time we exaggerate what we've done or said, we're not telling the truth. And believe me, our kids know it. If they don't see it when they're younger, they'll figure it out in their own therapy years later!

I believe this is what Jesus was referring to when he taught his followers to keep it simple. "Let your yays be yays and your nays be nays." In order to know what to do next, we have to tell the truth about what we're doing now. In order to move forward with purpose and passion, we need to tell the truth about where we are.

Here's how it can look with our kids. Our daughter came home her sophomore year of high school with a less than glowing progress report in German. This is a bright girl, with a proclivity for languages. Yet she was pulling a "D" in German. When questioned, the excuses poured forth. "Herr

Hoffman doesn't like me. I'm not good at German. And I'm not nearly as smart as you think I am!" Trying not to laugh, we gently and firmly continued to probe. "Did you study for your tests?" "Yes." "Do you participate in class?" "Yes." "Did you do all your homework?" Silence. "Honey, did you do all your homework?" "No." "Did you do most of your homework?" "No." "Could this be the reason you're getting a 'D' in German?" "Yes." Relief. The truth. "So what do you think you need to do to raise your grade in German?" "Do my homework."

This is a perfect example of the truth setting us free. Once we tell the truth, we know what to do. Actions based on the truth, on the facts, are REAL - relevant, effective, authentic and life-giving.

> "The snow goose need not bathe to make itself white. Neither need you do anything but be yourself."
> ~ Lao-Tse

Let's take a closer look at each of these components. *Relevant actions* are actions that are appropriate to the situation at hand. We take action based on what's happening in this moment, without worrying or obsessing over what we might or might not have done in the past. We take action based on what is presenting itself to us *right now*.

*Effective actions* are actions that produce a desired result. Sometimes a desired result is to allow a natural consequence to take effect. Sometimes we define the parameters more narrowly - "If this behavior continues, this will be the result."

*Authentic actions* are actions that are based on who we are, who we *truly* are. We all bring qualities to our interactions that are uniquely "us." For example, I tend to communicate in an informal, humorous manner. If I suddenly started sharing information in a professorial way, that would not be genuine. It would not be authentic. When we take actions, we need to take them the way WE do, not the way our parents would have, or our spouse would, or the current expert tells us to. We need to bring who we are to the situation and contribute as only we can.

*Life-giving actions* support us in living fully, and in moving forward. They empower and equip us, and those we love, to step up to life. They encourage us to take full responsibility for our choices and the outcomes they produce, and to embrace life with enthusiasm.

How do we know if our actions are REAL? When we are taking actions that are relevant, effective, authentic and life-giving, we will experience a loving detachment from their outcome. We will see ourselves and our families as capable human beings, willing and able to make our own decisions. We will experience a quiet joy, a deep satisfaction, within our relationships. Our interactions will become lighter, as we let go of our expectations of what all this should look like, and learn to be with, and learn from, what just IS.

*"If you do not tell the truth about yourself, you can't tell it about other people."*
*~ Virginia Woolf*

Oh, how right you are, Virginia! Always, when we speak of telling the truth, we are referring to telling the truth about ourselves. Because, ultimately, it is the only truth we can tell. As parents, it is one of the greatest gifts we can give our children. I believe more pain, suffering and heartache occur when we don't tell the truth, than when we do. Nowhere have I seen this more clearly than in my own family.

In telling the truth about myself, I needed to own that my guilt over decisions made in the past was causing me to not make good decisions in the present. This became painfully clear when our son Jon moved home after living with his father for several years. His return was predicated by an addiction to drugs and was ostensibly to help him clean up and "get back on his feet."

So what was the truth? The truth was that I was trying to alleviate 20 years of guilt and was enabling Jon to stay an addict. I had guilt over my divorce from his father, guilt over my feelings of frustration with Jon's "under achieving," guilt over the tension between him and his stepfather and siblings, guilt over my relief when he chose to stay with his father when we moved... guilt upon guilt upon guilt, all to be washed away by my allowing Jon to move home and be "fixed."

The truth was also that, yes, I had made mistakes with Jon, with all three of my children. And

I had also done a lot well. This is a critical element in our being willing to tell the truth. Tell it all. I was totally focused on everything I had done "wrong," and oblivious to all I had done "right." My guilt was blinding me to the many successes my children had enjoyed and to the closeness of our relationships. There was copious evidence that we had been "good parents" but I wasn't willing to see it. My guilt had made me blind. My guilt was holding me hostage to the past and preventing me from being fully present to what was happening under my own roof.

The truth was also that Jon was accountable for his own choices. At 20 years old, he needed to start taking responsibility for his actions. This was huge for me. As I agonized for almost a year over what to do, thoroughly frustrating the rest of my family, I finally had to tell the truth that I was not responsible for decisions that Jon was making as an adult. I finally had to allow him to experience the natural consequences of his behavior, and to see him as capable of dealing with those consequences.

Having told the truth, how did my actions become REAL? They became *relevant* when I was able to distinguish between my opinions about what Jon was doing - fed by my guilt over his decisions - and what he was actually doing. The fact was that he was taking substances into his body that were harmful to him, and causing him to behave in ways that were not beneficial to our family.

They became *effective* when I got very clear about what would happen if Jon did not choose to change his behavior. Their effectiveness was evidenced by results. Because he chose to continue drug-taking, he was asked to leave our home.

I was being *authentic* because my actions were true to who I am. I was clear, loving, gentle and firm. When I was finally able to tell the truth and let go of my guilt over every mistake I had ever made while Jon was growing up, I was able to communicate with him in a way that supported him in making his own decisions, and got me out of his way. I did not judge him, nor did I enable him.

And my actions were *life-giving* because I stopped reacting from the past and started responding in the present. I stopped seeing Jon as someone needing to be fixed and started to see him as a young man on his own journey. No, this was not a path I would have chosen for him. But it was his path to choose. Once I could see this and let go, everyone was able to move forward.

Did Jon stop taking drugs because I got REAL? No. After three rounds of hospitalization and rehab, our getting REAL resulted in Jon moving out. This was not an easy decision to make, as any parent who has struggled with an addicted child will tell you. But I got to see that my guilt, my ambivalence, was not helping Jon, and was causing significant stress and anxiety within my other family members. Regardless of the mistakes I had made, Jon's behavior was, in the moment, harmful to himself and stressful to the rest of our family. Regardless of how much I wanted him to make other choices, the truth was that he was not.

Are you jumping over yourself as if you weren't there, in the hope of finding a better

> "We can drop the fundamental hope that there is a better 'me' who one day will emerge. We can't just jump over ourselves as if we were not there."
> ~ Pema Chodron

you? Tell the truth. What does the chatter in your head say, the proverbial "Greek chorus" that comments on our every thought, our every action?

Are we willing to tell the ultimate Truth - that we are whole and complete? That we were born worthy, or in the words of Matthew Fox, that we were born with Original Blessing? Are we willing to let go of our fears and insecurities and tell the truth about our gifts and talents? Are we willing to embrace our responsibilities, or as Eric Butterworth observes, "our response to God's abilities"?

Are we willing to tell the truth about what has held us back? Are we willing to remove the obstacles, release old ways of thinking and embrace the unique contribution we have come here to make? And, are we willing to encourage our children to do the same? "You will know the truth and the truth will set you free." When you are willing to tell the truth about your wonderfulness, you will be free to live the life you've always dreamed of. And to be the parent of your children's dreams.

# The Fifth Promise:

## We promise to be grateful.

*"Gratitude unlocks the fullness of life. It turns what we have into enough, and more. It turns denial into acceptance, chaos to order, confusion to clarity. It can turn a meal into a feast, a house into a home, a stranger into a friend. Gratitude makes sense of our past, brings peace for today, and creates a vision for tomorrow." ~ Melody Beattie*

So what does gratitude have to do with being a guilt-free mother? Everything! "Gratitude makes sense of our past, brings peace for today, and creates a vision for tomorrow." When we are willing to look at our past from a grateful perspective, we are able to move into peaceful days of joyous mothering.

Much has been written about gratitude. Foster McClellan taught, "The kingdom of heaven is activated by our praise and thanksgiving; it responds to thankfulness." Myrtle Fillmore, co-founder of the Unity movement, states, "Praise and thanksgiving have within them the quickening spiritual power that produces growth and increase."

Studies have shown that gratitude is actually good for us. Recent research shows that:

~ People who describe themselves as feeling grateful to others and either to God or to the Universe in general tend to have higher vitality and more optimism, suffer less stress and experience less depression than the population as a whole. These results hold even when researchers factor out such things as age, health, and income, equalizing for the fact that the young, the well-to-do or the hale and hearty might have "more to be grateful for."

~ Grateful people tend to be less materialistic than the population as a whole and to suffer less anxiety about status or the accumulation of possessions. Partly because of this, they are more likely to describe themselves as happy or satisfied with life.

~ In an experiment with college students, those who kept a "gratitude journal," a weekly record of things they should feel grateful for, achieved better physical health, were more optimistic, exercised more regularly, and described themselves as happier than a control group of students who kept no journals but had the same overall measures of health, optimism, and exercise when the experiment began.

~ Grateful people are more spiritually aware and more likely to appreciate the interconnectedness of all life, regardless of whether they belong to specific religions.

*"All I have seen teaches me to trust the creator*
*for all I have not seen."*
*~ Emerson*

Gratitude also keeps us firmly focused on the good in our lives. One of my personal heroes knew this to be true at a cellular level and lived her life accordingly. That hero was Pollyanna, as portrayed in the movie by the same name. Unfortunately, Pollyanna has gotten a bad wrap. We tend to label people as "pollyannish" when we think they're not being realistic or seeing the world through "rose-colored glasses." In truth, Pollyana was one tough little girl. Pollyanna wasn't naive or protected from reality. She was the daughter of missionaries, dependent upon the charity of their home church to survive. She wore hand-me-down clothing, and was never guaranteed a meal.

Once, she opened up a missionary barrel expecting to find a doll. Instead, a pair of crutches was sent by mistake. It was at this point that her father invented the Glad Game. The point of the game was to become glad, to find the good, in any situation that presented itself. They finally decided that the good thing about receiving the crutches was that they didn't need to use them! Pollyanna made a choice to see the good in her life, to view people and situations as opportunities to do good in her life.

In a particularly poignant scene, she happened upon the local minister (played by Karl Malden), a real "fire and brimstoner." She showed him a locket worn by her father before his death, with an inscription by Abraham Lincoln: *"When you look for the bad in mankind, expecting to find it, you surely will."* This led her father to realize that the opposite was also true - that if you look for the good, you will surely find it. He began a search and found over 800 references in the Bible to joy and gladness (826 to be exact). Expressing gratitude is recognizing the potential for joy in every experience.

Gratitude helps us recognize that everything that has happened in our life has brought us to now. Kahlil Gibran expresses this so beautifully: "Your joy is your sorrow unmasked. And the selfsame well from which your laughter rises was oftentimes filled with your tears." Gratitude helps us to see that our joy is our sorrow unmasked. As Cicero once observed, gratitude is the parent of all other virtues - love, patience, kindness, joy. It's hard to be sad or depressed or resentful when you insist on seeing the good in every situation, when you insist on being grateful for whatever shows up in your life, when you insist on trusting the creator, on trusting the process. This is what helped the college students in the study to describe themselves as happy and content with their lives. This was the power behind Pollyanna.

And this can be the power behind our parenting. What would it be like to become grateful for everything in our lives, and in our children's lives? What if we would shift from "Why did this happen?" to

"There's a lesson here - and I'm open to learning it." This can be a challenge, particularly when what is happening was not part of our plan! I was given the opportunity to practice this shift when our son Collin decided, as a college senior, that his major no longer interested him and he wanted to take some time off from school to decide what did interest him. I will confess that I initially panicked. What if he never went back to school? How was he going to pay the student loans that would now become due? What would our family think? Only when I shifted to becoming grateful for his clarity, and releasing his outcome, was I able to be present to him and support his decision.

> "Gratitude for the abundance you have received is the best insurance that the abundance will continue."
> ~ Muhammed

One of the big lessons I needed to learn as a parent of three born-very-close-together children was to allow them to be frustrated. As I confessed earlier, my inclination was always to jump in and fix whatever was bothering them. Obviously, when our children are infants we need to respond immediately to their needs. This fosters a sense of security and certainty that is important for their development. And, as they get older, starting when they are toddlers and into their early childhood years, I have come to believe that we need to allow them to be occasionally frustrated in their efforts.

Why? First, to learn that being frustrated is a temporary occurrence. Even as adults, we tend to think that our frustration will last forever. The earlier we learn that "this too shall pass" the easier our lives will be. Second, because we frequently learn the most from that which doesn't come quickly to us, from that which causes us to break a little sweat. Gary Simmons, in his book *The I of the Storm*, calls this being at the "edge of our resourcefulness."

When we are at the edge of our resourcefulness, we are at the limit of what we currently know. We are on the brink of learning a new thing, or a new way of being. This can demonstrate as frustration. When we as parents can see our children's frustration as their being on the brink of learning a new thing, or discovering something amazing about themselves, we can move into a place of gratitude for that frustration. We can support them in their learning and growth, rather than trying to fix what really isn't broken.

One word of caution here when dealing with a teenager's frustration: Experience your gratitude quietly to yourself, as they are probably not going to be very receptive to you seeing their frustration as anything other than a terribly dramatic and personal crisis! Discretion is always the better part of valor. And once the current crisis has passed, you may want to use it as an opportunity to have a quiet conversation about what they've learned.

*"Finally beloved, whatever is true, whatever is honorable, whatever is just, whatever is pure, whatever is pleasing, whatever is commendable, if there is any excellence and if there is anything worthy of praise, think about these things. Keep on doing these things and the God of peace will be with you." ~ Philippians 4:8-9*

"Think about these things." It sounds so easy! And yet I have found that my focus tends to veer towards those thing that aren't going so well. One tool I have used to keep my focus on things "worthy of praise" is to keep a Gratitude Journal. There's nothing like counting your blessings every night before going to sleep to set a positive tone for the next day.

Sarah Ban Breathnach, author of *Simple Abundance*, suggests writing down five things that you can be grateful for every night. She acknowledges that some days they'll be the "big" things - a promotion, a new car, a birth, or your dog learning a new trick. And some days, it's hard to come up with five "little" things. Those are the days it's most important to write in your journal. Those are the days you put down those things that we take for granted - our health, our families, the subway running on time, our car starting, the smile of a child or an "I love you honey" as your partner walks out the door for work.

She observes, "The gratitude journal is not an option. Why? Because you simply will not be the same person two months from now after consciously giving thanks each day for the abundance that exists in your

78

life. And you will have set in motion an ancient spiritual law: the more you have and are grateful for, the more will be given you." I would add we will not be the same parents two months from now if we consciously give thanks each day for everything in our children's lives.

> *"I don't want the peace that passeth understanding. I want the understanding that brings peace."* ~ *Helen Keller*

During a discussion at my church, I asked the question, "What makes you feel peaceful?" The responses were many and varied. I was particularly interested in one participant's response, "I feel peaceful when I can be grateful for, and present to, the moment." As we explored this response, I saw how this practice not only combines two of our promises - to be present and to be grateful - but takes the synthesis of the two to a level of peace in our lives that can't help but move us into a place of joyous mothering. When we can be grateful for it all, whatever that "all" may be, we are modeling for our children, and our world, an understanding that will bring peace.

# The Sixth Promise:
## We promise to be loving.

*"Love given is love received."*
*~ John Marks Templeton*

We promise to be loving. This would seem to be a given. Of course we love our children, sometimes it feels like more than life itself. Wouldn't we do anything to ensure their happiness and wellbeing, to ensure their safety? We want our children to know how loved they are, how very dear they are to us, and we show that love with affection, care, support and gifts.

We also show that love, on occasion, with discipline and natural consequences. As my father used to say to us when we had clearly crossed the line, "I need to prove to you how much I love you." As a child, and especially as a teenager, I didn't get that, but as a parent, I understand completely. In healthy families, it brings parents no pleasure to have to discipline a child, or to allow them to suffer the natural consequences of their actions, but it is often the most loving thing a parent can do.

With each of our children, we have had the occasion to stand back and allow them to learn from their mistakes. From the outside, it would appear that our actions were not loving, that we should have jumped in and "saved" them. But we knew, in our hearts if not always in our heads, that they were capable, and that these situations were immense learning opportunities for them - and for us. We were all learning just how resourceful we could be, and how powerful a teacher experience is.

> "Put the oxygen mask on yourself first."
> ~ ancient airline wisdom

I have also learned the importance of loving myself. As I shared earlier, for years I suffered under the delusion that being a "good" mother meant that I should put my needs last, always focused on the needs of my children first. Unfortunately, this can, and in my case did, lead not to being a loving mother, but to being a martyr. I am very grateful to my husband for encouraging me to see the importance of putting the oxygen mask on myself first.

Although something I had heard for years in my travels, it never occurred to me that there was wisdom here beyond the flight attendant's instructions. Why do we put the oxygen mask on ourself first? Clearly so we don't pass out! And just as clearly, so we can take care of those around us. When we don't make sure our needs are met, we're no good to anyone, least of all those we love the most.

Once the oxygen mask was on, I started to look at my concept of what it meant to be "loving." What I saw wasn't pretty. Because what I saw was that I was trying to love my children into liking me. I thought if my children became upset or angry, I had done something wrong, something "unloving." I took their reactions personally. I made their discomfort my own. I felt a keen, and often heavy, sense of responsibility for my children and their behavior. Isn't that what loving mothers did - assume responsibility for their children's behavior?

And then I was challenged to examine that belief. During my coaching training, I was invited to replace the word "responsibility" with the word "privilege." Was I willing to shift my thinking around what it meant to be "responsible?" Was I willing to see these relationships and tasks as a privilege? The results were transformative. No longer did I see loving, and taking care of, my children as a responsibility. Loving them became a privilege. No longer were their responses seen as an indicator of how I was doing. It became a privilege to support them in their growth. Putting on the oxygen mask first became a loving gesture.

I began to see that to be truly loving meant to let go of my expectations of what I thought their lives should look like, what I thought being a "good mother" looked like. Does this mean there wasn't, and doesn't continue to be, room for growth, maturity and change? Of course not. But seeing my children as fine just they way they were created the space for that growth, maturity and change to occur.

*"If your willingness to give blessings is limited, so also is your ability to receive them. This is the subtle operation of the Tao."*

*~ Hua Hu Ching, Lao Tzu*

Think about your own life. When did your biggest shifts happen? When you were in relationships filled with disapproval and reproach? Or when you were in the presence of someone who saw you as capable and willing? There has been some research done that illustrates what happens when we are in the presence of such positive regard. It appears that we release the hormone oxytocin in our body as a physiological response to being held in high esteem. This is the same hormone released when mothers breast feed, which elicits a calming effect from the mother.

In other words, our body responds positively to being seen in a positive light, to being loved. It only stands to reason that the opposite is also true - we respond negatively when we sense that we are seen in a negative way. Think about the ramifications of this finding. When we see our children positively,

84

they will be more open to exploring the possibilities, less fearful, more curious, and more confident in their abilities. When we stop seeing our children as reflections of who we are, they have the freedom to be fully who they are.

*"You may give them your love but not your thoughts, for they have their own thoughts."*
~ *Kahlil Gibran*

Oh, how we want to give our children our thoughts! As my husband observes, "If only everyone would think the way we do, everything would be fine!" But of course the truth is, everyone doesn't. And something I've observed is that it's easier to love those who think the way we do, including our children. It's easier to be loving with someone who agrees with us, who validates our opinions, who may even seek out our advice. Who doesn't love that? The challenge, and ultimately the growth, comes when we're willing to love equally those who don't agree, to be loving towards those who don't share our opinions or our expectations.

The Buddhists call this loving detachment. This is a benevolent and unconditional love, a love unconcerned with a specific outcome, or our personal desires. Dr. Wayland Myers describes it this way: "I consider myself lovingly detached when I am willing and able to compassionately, and without judgment, allow others to be different from me, allow them to be self-directed, and allow them to be responsible for taking care of themselves." If we continue our previous word substitution here, "to allow them *the privilege* of taking care of themselves."

Literally, to *be detached* means to be not joined or connected. Interestingly, we sometimes make detachment mean a lack of caring. Loving detachment is quite the opposite. Contrary to not caring, loving detachment allows us to care about everything, without being joined or connected to it. Rather than limiting our love to a few "special" recipients, loving detachment allows us to care about everything, and everyone, without exception. Because we are willing to be present to what is, without attachment to what might be, we are free to love with open hearts and open minds.

*"To love is, above all, to be there."*
*~Thich Nhat Hanh*

To be loving is to be willing "to be there" even in the presence of our own discomfort or busy-ness or judgments, to be willing to truly love without conditions or expectations. And, if we believe Jesus, this also means that we are willing to love our children *as ourselves*. Remember the oxygen mask? We know in the coaching and therapeutic professions that we cannot take a client past where we ourselves have not been willing to go. This is particularly relevant with regard to this promise. In fact, one of the prerequisites of loving detachment is self-acceptance.

Pema Chodron observes in her lovely little book, *Awakening Loving-Kindness*, that the object of directing loving kindness towards ourselves "doesn't mean getting rid of anything. The point is not to try to change ourselves. It's about befriending who we are already." The promise to be loving is about loving who we are, loving who our children are, and in the loving, letting go of all that isn't.

*"Loving is as loving does."*
~ *Stephanie Moyer Seigh (yep, that's me!)*

The old adage "actions speak louder than words" is particularly true here. We can have all the loving thoughts and intentions in the world, but if we don't show the people we love how much we love them, our intentions don't mean much. To *be loving* is active, not passive.

We have always been an affectionate and verbally loving family. However, when Jon became a teenager, all of a sudden, hugging and "I love you" were not acceptable. When questioned about his new-found standoffishness, we began to understand that he now associated these displays of affection as only appropriate between romantic partners. As teenagers do, he was discovering his sexuality and had become uncomfortable with affection from his parents, especially from me.

At first, we dealt with this by backing off. But eventually, as Jon re-entered our lives and began his struggle with drugs and mental illness, we saw that our distance wasn't helping. We began to slowly reintroduce hugs and verbal "I love you's" to our now young-adult son. Although awkward at first, he responded more and more warmly, and now Jon never comes or goes without a hug and an "I love you."

We learned a big lesson from this experience. Yes, it's important to honor and respect where our kids are in their development. And it's also important to not let any "stage" prevent us from showing our children how much we love them. When Collin began to show the same discomfort around hugs and "I love you's," we didn't back off. We hugged him anyway, acknowledging his discomfort with gentle good humor, and when he left for college, we never ended a phone conversation without an "I love you, Collie." It took a while, but, just like Jon, eventually the hugs were returned and the "I love you too, Mom" was back.

*"Love possesses not nor would it be possessed;*
*For love is sufficient unto love."*
*~ Kahlil Gibran*

"Our children are not our own." This wisdom applies to this promise perhaps more than to all the others. To be loving is to acknowledge that we do not possess our children. One of the hardest things for me to learn as a mother was that other people were capable of loving my children. I wanted to believe that only I could really love them, that only I knew *how* to love them. But this simply wasn't, and isn't, true. I have seen many people love and care for my children over the years with a level of affection and concern that rivals my own.

In her book, *It Takes A Village*, Hillary Rodham Clinton observes, "Children exist in the world as well as in the family. From the moment they are born, they depend on a host of other 'grown-ups' – grandparents, neighbors, teachers, ministers, employers, political leaders, and untold others who touch their lives directly and indirectly... Each of us plays a part in every child's life: It takes a village to raise a child." I have been both humbled and grateful for the village that has raised my children. And I have seen that I am not the only person in their lives that knows how to love them. Sometimes the most loving thing we can do is to allow another to love our children.

Not only is this good for them, it's good for us. When my children were very young, I frequently experienced anxiety over what would happen to them if something happened to me. I was convinced that if my life ended, so would theirs. After all, I was their mother – no one could love them more, no one knew what was best for them like I did. Fortunately for us all, this was not true. Not only have my friends and family loved my children, but they have exposed them to experiences and worlds beyond my scope.

Their grandparents have literally taken them across the country and around the world. Their father has taken them hiking, camping and mountain climbing - something Ken and I are not about to attempt soon! Our friends, and theirs, have introduced them to books, music and political ideas outside of our own. Their teachers, heroes all, have supported them in going beyond where they thought themselves capable. And we have shared with them our love of the arts, fine food, spirituality, and, of course, keeping our promises. I have seen that to be loving is to allow others to love, and to be loved, by my children. And in that allowing, my children have learned that they can be, and are, loved by any village they create, for "love is sufficient unto love."

# The Seventh Promise:

## We promise to forgive.

*"At a certain point, we forgive because we decide to forgive. Healing occurs in the present, not the past. We are not held back by the love we didn't receive in the past, but by the love we're not extending in the present."*

~ Marianne Williamson

I love *Star Trek*. I have given many sermons on the metaphysics of *Star Trek* and find great wisdom among the various series' incarnations. From the original series to *The Next Generation*, *Deep Space Nine*, *Voyager* and finally *Enterprise*, I have been educated and enlightened through the writing and production of this amazing franchise. Gene Roddenberry had a vision. He saw *Star Trek* as a vehicle to express his view of a utopian future, where prejudice and greed were things of the past, and everyone was valued for what they had to offer, not the color of their skin or their country - or planet - of origin.  Dr. King would have been proud.

And yet, even in this utopian view of our future, we find the guilt-ridden mother. In a poignant episode of *Star Trek: The Next Generation* entitled "The Dark Page," we are introduced to a telepathic race called the Cairn.  Ship's counselor, Deanna Troi's mother, Lwaxana Troi, has been assisting the race to learn to speak verbally.  When she arrives on the Enterprise with the Cairn delegation, Deanna notices that her mother seems unusually tired and drawn. When questioned, Lwaxana reassures Deanna that she is just feeling the effects of being in constant telepathic communication with the leader of the Cairn delegation.

Still concerned, Deanna questions the leader, Maques.  He observes about Lwaxana that, "Always there is a part of her that is dark." As Deanna probes further, she believes that he is referring to the concept of privacy, something foreign to the telepathic race.

As the episode continues, Lwaxana collapses

and falls into a deep coma, retreating into her metaconscious mind. As Dr. Crusher struggles to understand what is happening to her patient, Deanna explains that the metaconscious mind in Betazeds (her mother's race) is the part of the mind that filters information, and in particular the area that filters out trauma.

Puzzled as to what could have caused this reaction, Deanna contacts her mother's friends and associates, and pours over her personal journals. Nothing explains her mother's condition, until she goes back to the beginning of her parent's marriage and finds that shortly after Deanna's birth, Lwaxana has deleted seven years of her personal journal entries.

Now thoroughly confused, and as a last resort, Deanna enters into her mother's mind in an attempt to discover what she has been suppressing. Maques warns Deanna that her mother is very afraid and will try to stop her from discovering the truth. As Deanna travels through the corridors of her mother's mind, Lwaxana throws up barriers in the forms of memories and fears from Deanna's past. But Deanna perseveres and eventually walks into the darkness, literally stepping into the void of her mother's metaconscious mind.

There she finds an idyllic scene, with her parents picnicking by the side of a lake. Deanna sees herself as an infant, and someone she doesn't recognize: an older child, a seven-year-old, whom her mother calls Kestra. Deanna quickly realizes that this young girl is her sister - a sister she never knew existed. In this poignant scene, Lwaxana starts to weep, imploring Deanna to not make her see this again. Deanna insists, asking her mother to remember. "You have to remember. You can't hold it back. It's killing you."

As the scene unfolds, Deanna watches as Lwaxana re-lives Kestra wandering off, following their wayward puppy, and drowning in the nearby lake. As Lwaxana sobs into Deanna's arms, she asks, "Why did I look away?" Deanna, herself in tears, comforts her mother. "You have to forgive yourself, Mother. You have to let it go."

"How can I?" laments Lwaxana. "I let her die."

Deanna continues to reassure her. "It was a terrible tragedy, the worst thing that can happen to a parent. I know you feel responsible, but it was an accident. And what you're doing isn't fair to Kestra. I saw a little girl who was sweet and happy. She must have brought a great deal of joy to your lives. Isn't it better to remember her like that? I just found out I had a sister I never knew. I'd like to learn what was good and joyous about her, to celebrate her life, not mourn it."

"How can I do that?" moans Lwaxana. "Kestra was here a few moments ago," replied Deanna. "Talk to her."

"No, I can't," cried Lwaxana. Firmly, Deanna tells her, "Do it, Mother. Tell her how you feel. I'll be here with you. I'll help you."

Kestra appears again, facing Lwaxana, who takes her in her arms. "Kestra, my precious one, I am so sorry." After a moment's embrace, Kestra tells Lwaxana, "I have to go now, Mommy." As Kestra disappears before their eyes, Deanna and Lwaxana take hands... and wake up from their sleep.

There are so many lessons to be learned from this episode. To paraphrase the gospel of Thomas, "If you bring forth what is within you, what you have will save you. If you do not bring forth that which is within you, what you do not have within you will kill you." I usually call upon this verse to illustrate the importance of showing up authentically, of fully sharing our gifts and talents. However, this story begs a different interpretation.

What Lwaxana is denying, the memories she is suppressing, the memories she is refusing to bring forth, are literally killing her. By refusing to acknowledge Kestra's existence, the grief she has tried to ignore is consuming her life. And the darkness that is "always with her" has doused her light. Deanna recognizes this when she tells her mother that she wants to hear about what was good and joyous about Kestra, to celebrate her life. By focusing on the tragedy of Kestra's death, Lwaxana had denied herself, and Deanna, the joyful memories that were a part of Kestra's life.

98

> *"Forgiveness does not change the past, but it does enlarge the future."*
> ~Paul Boese

How often we do this - allow our regrets to prevent us from celebrating our joys. We allow the events of the past to keep us from being present to the present. Are we willing to let go? Or have we become comfortable with our regrets? While this may sound counter-intuitive or even masochistic, it happens. We can become resigned to our grief, as Lwaxana had done. It takes courage to face our past, to tell the truth about what we did or didn't do, and to let go.

Maques warned Deanna before she entered her mother's metaconscious mind that it would be a struggle. Her mother's mind had grown accustomed to blocking the memories, and threw up obstacles on Deanna's path to prevent her from discovering the truth. We may not have the metaconscious mind of the Betazeds, but our minds can be very effective nevertheless at preventing us from seeing whatever we are denying. Facing our decisions is a conscious choice and it is the first step towards true forgiveness.

What are you holding onto, right now, that is limiting the flow of joy in your life? Are you willing to let it go? Do you have the courage to release the past and embrace the present? Are you willing to do whatever it takes to live life fully, to let go of any fear or resentment that is keeping you "stuck"? Are you willing to let go of the pain?

*"Forgiving someone means making a conscious choice to let go of the pain, to let go of the need to be right, and to allow yourself to heal and to be happy instead. Forgiveness is an act of consciously seeing everyone blessed for their highest good in the situation that is grieving you."*

*~ Paula Langguth Ryan*

*A Course in Miracles* teaches that forgiveness is recognizing that what you thought had occurred never happened. Sounds interesting, but what does that really mean? One possible interpretation could be that what we *thought* happened never occurred, emphasis on what we *thought*, i.e. our opinion of what happened. When we release our judgment of what has happened as "bad" or "good," forgiveness occurs. When we let go of what we made the occurrence mean, forgiveness occurs. When we are willing to "see everyone blessed" by the situation, forgiveness occurs.

Could it be that forgiveness also occurs when we are willing to acknowledge that everyone is doing their best? When I look at some of the decisions I made when my children were young, I cringe. Yet at the time, I was doing the best I could, with the resources, skills and experience I had at the time. This knowledge has also allowed me to be forgiving of my parents and some of their decisions. They too were doing the best they could at the time.

When we are able to apply this knowing to everyone in our lives, that at any given moment we are all doing the best we can *in that moment*, we are free from the events and judgments of our past. David Owen Ritz observes that, "Forgiveness begins when you decide that you no longer want to carry your negative feelings along with you. This step requires a genuine willingness to heal and let go."

*"Trials are but lessons that you failed to learn
presented once again, so where you made a
faulty choice before you now can make
a better one."*
~ A Course in Miracles

Do you see a theme developing here? Letting go. Are we willing to learn from our mistakes, be spacious around our learning process, and then LET GO! I once had a therapist point out to me the arrogance of my regrets. Ouch. She asked if I thought I was the only person who had ever made a mistake. Who did I think I was to presume that I alone among women had screwed up occasionally with my kids? I was forced to confront the self-centeredness of my wallowing and to see how it wasn't serving anyone - martyrdom rarely does.

We have taught our children since they were very young to focus on the positive, to count their blessings. I was being a lousy role model by focusing on my mistakes and not celebrating my successes as a mother. I needed to forgive myself for those mistakes and let go of my pain and regret so I could be fully present to my children now. I had to let go of the mother I had been so I could be the mother I had become.

> "The (newspaper) clipping said forgiveness meant that God is *for giving, and that we are here* for giving too, and that to withhold love or blessings is to be completely delusional."
> ~From Traveling Mercies by Anne Lamott

Oh, Anne, how true that is! When we are unwilling to forgive ourselves and others, we stop the flow of love and blessings in our lives. Because Lwaxana was unwilling to forgive herself for Kestra's death, she had withheld all knowledge of Kestra, and the blessings she would have received from that knowledge, from Deanna. She also denied herself the blessing of the memories she had of the seven years she had lived with and loved Kestra.

How many blessings have we denied ourselves because we have refused to accept, and extend, forgiveness? Keeping this promise entails first and foremost being willing to be *for giving*. Are we willing to be generous with our selves and others, recognizing that we will all make mistakes? That we are all doing our best? To be truly *for giving* means that we are willing to focus on learning from our mistakes, not focusing on them. It means making amends and apologies when necessary, letting go and moving on. To be truly *for giving* allows us to see that we are all learning as we go along, to genuinely enjoy our families... and finally, to step into being a Joyous Mother.

# The Joyous Mother

*"If you want to know my definition
of hell,  it's having children and
thinking there is such a thing as
a good parent."*
~ *Marshall Rosenberg*

And so our journey has come full circle, through
the promises - to be present, to lighten up, to be
kind, to tell the truth, to be grateful, loving and
forgiving - to a definition of hell.  An interesting way
to start this, our final chapter.   And yet, it is
appropriate, for heaven and hell are ultimately states
of mind... and we can change our mind.  We can
choose to be in heaven.   We can choose to be a
Joyous Mother.

Ultimately,    making    and    keeping    these
promises, or any promise, is a choice.  Every day,
every hour, every minute we are faced with choices.
The choices we make in this minute determine the
choices we are presented with in the next minute.

Guilt is a choice.  Perfectionism is a choice.  Shame, regret, blame, resentment, judgment are all choices we can make.  And so are joy, acceptance, kindness, gentleness, generosity and compassion.  To paraphrase Rosenberg, "If you want to know my definition of heaven, it's having children and knowing there is no such thing as a good parent!"

Why is this important?  Because if in one moment we think, "Here I was a *good* parent," in the next moment we might, in comparison, think, "There I was a *bad* parent."  A kinder, gentler way of looking at it might be, "There I did the best I could, and I am willing to learn."  In the absence of labeling and judging our parenting, we are actually freed up to be more effective, and more joyous,  parents.

> *"Joy has to do with seeing how big,*
> *how completely unobstructed,*
> *and how precious things are."*
> ~ *Pema Chodron*

I love this approach to joy, because it's not about what's happening that determines our joy, it's about how we're seeing what's happening. From this perspective, joy is an inside job.  Does this mean we'll never feel sad or frustrated or angry?  Of course not.  We'll continue to feel the gamut of our emotions.  Stuff happens.  And we get to decide how we're going to respond to that stuff.

Our children may or may not like our decisions.  Our husbands, parents, friends, and colleagues may or may not agree with us on a myriad of topics, not the least of which will be how to raise our children.  We can choose to be joyous in the presence of all of this, and more.  Even in the midst of tragedy - and sometimes even more so - we can choose to see how very precious things are.

We will make and break these promises many times.  In the words of William Jordan: "Let us be glad of the dignity of our privilege to make mistakes, glad of the wisdom that enables us to recognize them, glad of the power  that permits us to turn their light as a glowing  illumination along the pathway of our future.  Mistakes are the growing pains of wisdom. Without them there would be no individual growth, no progress, no conquest."

Let us be glad of the wisdom that enables us to recognize our mistakes, because we are going to make them. Lest we be naive, there are going to be days when we don't *feel* loving, just as there will be days when we don't *feel* like being kind or grateful or present, or any of the other promises. These are the days when we get to choose joy. These are the days when we get to acknowledge that everything but joy may be showing up... nevertheless, in the face of all evidence to the contrary, we choose to be joyous.

On these days, we may not be up to keeping all seven promises. Remember what happens when we make a promise? We enter into a state of tension that is only relieved when we keep the promise. So we feel good when we keep any of our promises, *large or small*. On these days, we can make just one small, sweet promise and in the keeping of it, reclaim our joy.

*"Your joy is your sorrow unmasked. And the selfsame well from which your laughter rises was oftentimes filled with your tears."*
*~ Kahlil Gibran*

Of all the wisdom of Kahlil Gibran that I have

enjoyed through the years, this is my favorite. We have all experienced sorrow in our lives to varying degrees. Tears are a normal, and sometimes necessary, part of life. And yet, as reflected in this passage from *The Prophet*, it is the very cause of our tears that can bring us the greatest joy. Our children are the most poignant example of this truth. My children have been the source of my greatest joy and my greatest sorrow.

Or perhaps more accurately, my *experience* of my children has been the cause of my greatest joy and my greatest sorrow. As much as we would like to believe otherwise, another human being cannot cause us to feel anything. This brings us back to choice. We always get to choose how we are going to respond to any situation. We always get to choose how we are going to respond to our children. We can respond with fear or we can respond with the calm assurance that all is well.

What will I focus my attention on - my mistakes or what I've learned from them? Gibran continues the above passage by asking, "And how else can it be?

The deeper that sorrow carves into your being, the more joy you can contain." Am I willing to accept the sorrow so I can hold more joy? This is a powerful question. To *accept* literally means to receive willingly or gladly. Am I willing to gladly receive it all - all the sorrow, all the joy, all the pain, all the gladness? Am I willing to be present to what is, to hold it lightly, to be kind in the face of frustration and anger, to tell the truth with courage, to be grateful without judgment, to love unconditionally - and to forgive gracefully when I don't?

We began our journey with wisdom from the Buddha: With our thoughts we create our world. For years, my thoughts were filled with grief and regret. "If only..." consumed my attention. For years, as I struggled to complete these pages, I was more interested in that grief than in what I could contribute. It was only when I was willing to be more interested in what I could offer that I was able to shift into a place of joy - into a place of contributing both to my children and to other mothers who might share my experiences.

*"Making the decision to have a child – it's wondrous. It is to decide forever to have your heart go walking around outside your body."*
~ *Elizabeth Stone*

I can truthfully say that the three days my children were born were the happiest three days of my life. Yes, it hurt. And that pain carved a place in my being that has held great joy. My children have been my greatest teachers. Through them, I have learned of myself. In my bearing of them, they have birthed a Mother. And I am indescribably proud of each of them. I love Jon, my firstborn, for making me a mom. I am proud of his sensitivity and creativity. He is a healer in the making. I love Collin for his sweetness. In his eyes, I see an ancient soul. I am proud of his intelligence, perseverance and compassion. I love Jackie, for she is the daughter I yearned for. I am proud of her wisdom, her courage and her sense of adventure. She is the Warrior Woman I have always wanted to be.

Through this journey, I have made, broken and kept these promises many times. And the journey continues. For now, I am more interested in loving and enjoying my children than in agonizing over the mistakes I have made, and will continue to make. For now, I am more interested in learning, loving and growing with them than I am in being "a good mother." For now, I choose joy.... and just for now, just for today, I hope you will join me.

*"You are the bows from which your children*
*as living arrows are sent forth.*
*The archer sees the mark upon the path of the*
*infinite, and He bends you with His might that*
*His arrows may go swift and far.*
*Let your bending in the archer's hand*
*be for gladness;*
*For even as He loves the arrow that flies,*
*so He loves also the bow that is stable."*
*~ Kahlil Gibran*

# Epilogue

*"It is as grandmothers
that our mothers come into
the fullness of their grace."*
~ Christopher Morley

While this manuscript was sitting on a shelf waiting to be born, another birth was taking place, on Mother's Day no less. Our granddaughter, Madalyn Elaine, was born to Jonathan and his friend, Alicia. Maddy is a blond-haired, blue-eyed bundle of joy that has transformed our lives. Pa-pa and Grammy Fifi, as Ken and I are now affectionately known, have become the quintessential doting grandparents to this amazing little girl.

And Christopher Morley was right. I have experienced a fullness of grace as a grandmother that has infused my mothering with new joy and a newfound perspective. I watch with pride as Jon takes care of his little girl, and with delight as Jackie has become "Aunt Yackie," embracing her new role with complete devotion. As our family has grown, so has our capacity to embrace the unexpected and to love with abandon. And the lessons we're learning from our little Maddy... but that's for another book, joyously written!

# About the Author

*"Be the change
you wish to see in the world."*
*~ Gandhi*

Rev. Stephanie M. Seigh, PCC, a self-proclaimed Air Force "brat," grew up around the country and the world. An ICF Certified Life Coach through the Academy for Coaching Excellence in Sacramento, CA, Stephanie is also an ordained Interfaith Minister and obtained a B.S. in biology from The Pennsylvania State University.

Currently, Stephanie is the Director of Peacemaking & Transitional Services for the Association of Unity Churches International. Professionally, she specializes in organizational growth and revitalization, and in facilitating joyous and effective leadership.

Personally, she   enjoys her family and supporting other mothers into loving themselves and their children... guilt-free!

2315522

Made in the USA